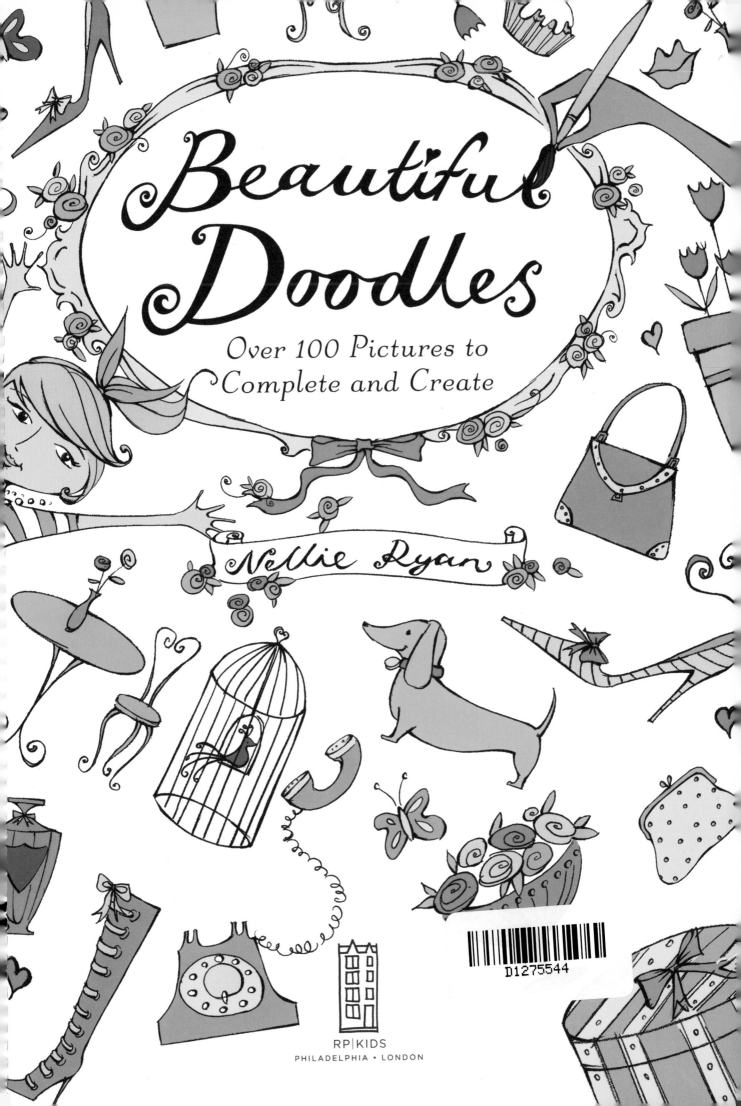

Beautiful Doodles

Over 100 Pictures to
Complete and Create

Nellie Ryan

RP|KIDS
PHILADELPHIA • LONDON

D1275544

Illustrated by Nellie Ryan for Charlotte and Sophie

ISBN 978-0-7624-5289-7

9 8 7 6 5 4 3 2 1
Digit on the right indicates the number of this printing

This edition published by:
Running Press Kids
An Imprint of Running Press Book Publishers
A Member of the Perseus Books Group
2300 Chestnut Street
Philadelphia, PA 19103–4371

Visit us on the web!
www.runningpress.com/kids

Furnish the doll's house.

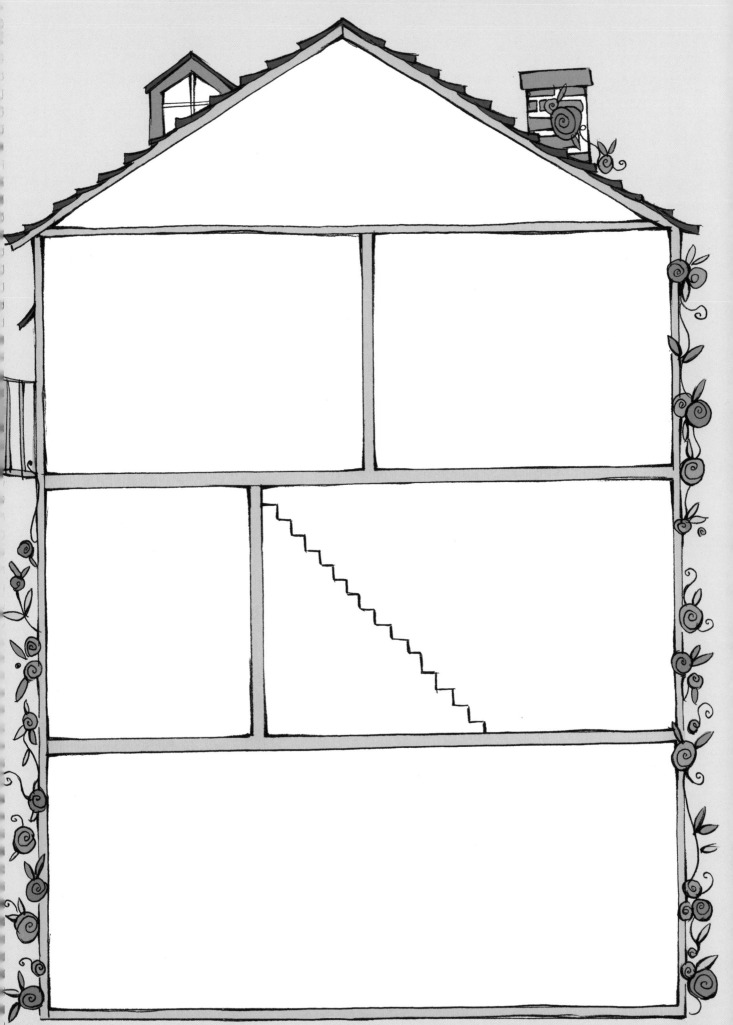

Fill the frames.

Decorate the fan.

What can you see in the crystal ball?

Decorate the paper doll's clothes.

What animals are in the pet shop?

What have you baked?

Bubbles everywhere!

Finish the dandelions.

Make our nails gorgeous.

Decorate the piggy bank.

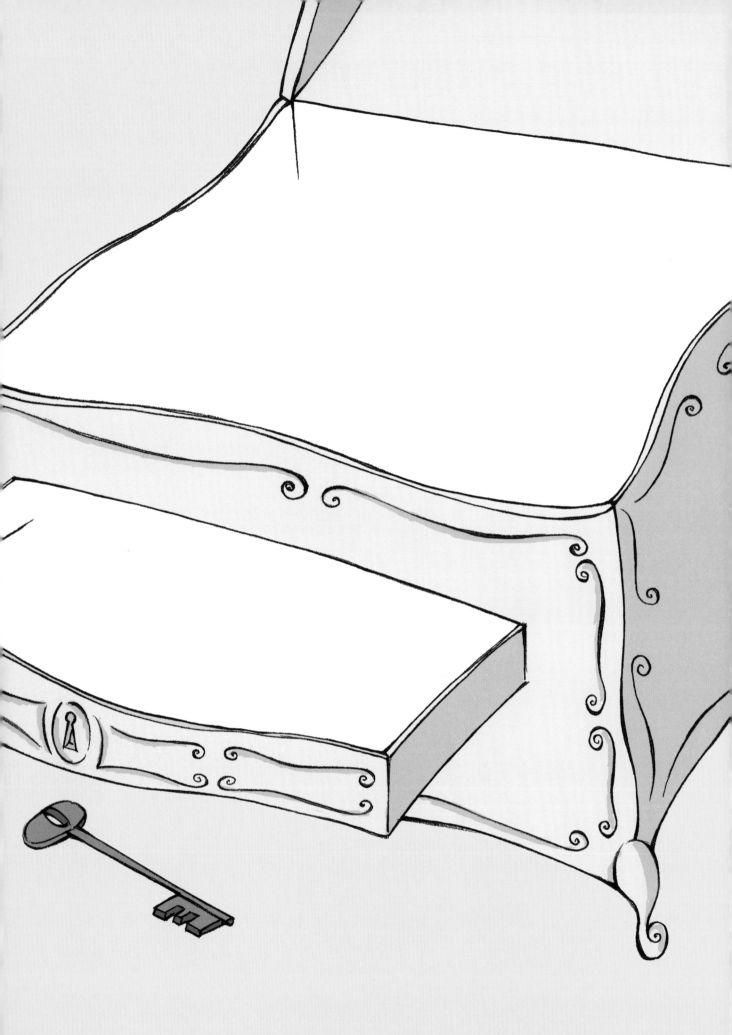

What beautiful jewelry!

What can you see out
of the window?

Hundreds of flowers.

Decorate the crowns.

Give the butterflies beautiful wings.

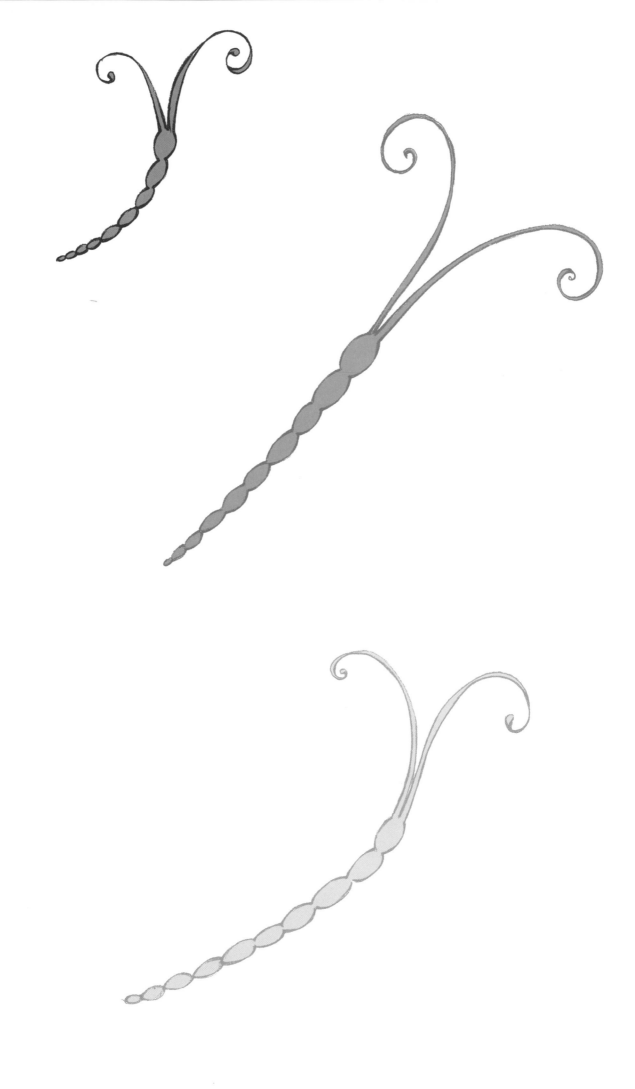

Decorate the masks.

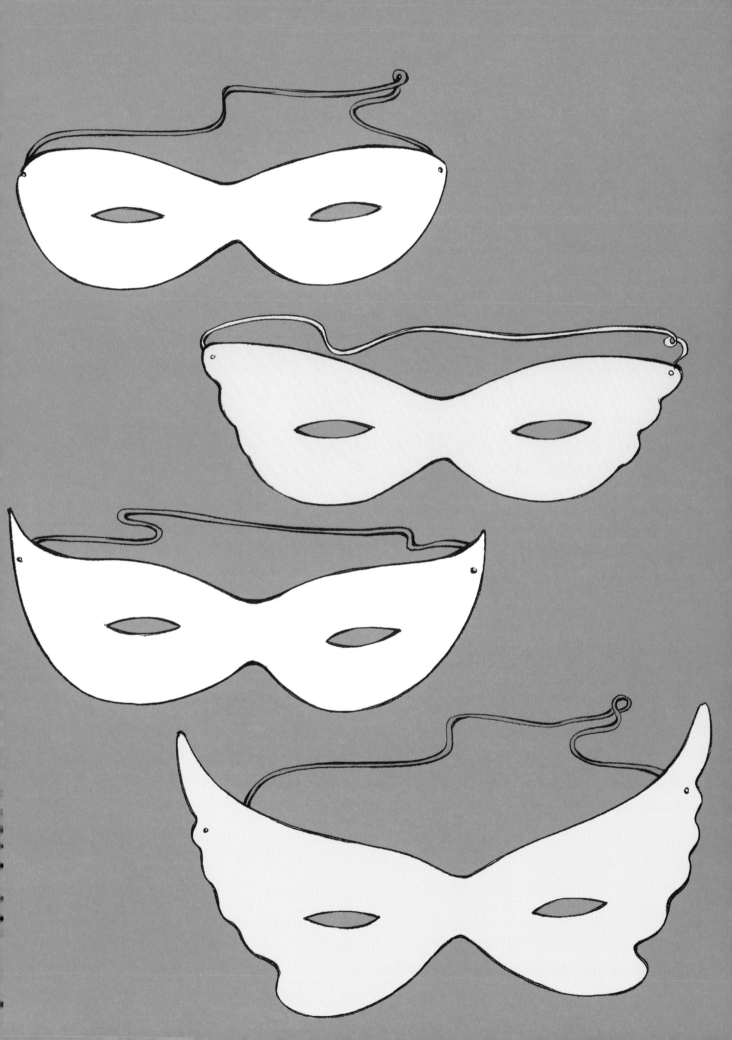

Arrange flowers in these vases.

Give me glamorous sunglasses and earrings.

Finish the shoes and fill the shop.

What kinds of chocolates are in the box?

Laundry day.

Decorate the cupcakes.

A fashionista's wardrobe.

Give the dog a designer outfit.

What can you conjure out of the hat?

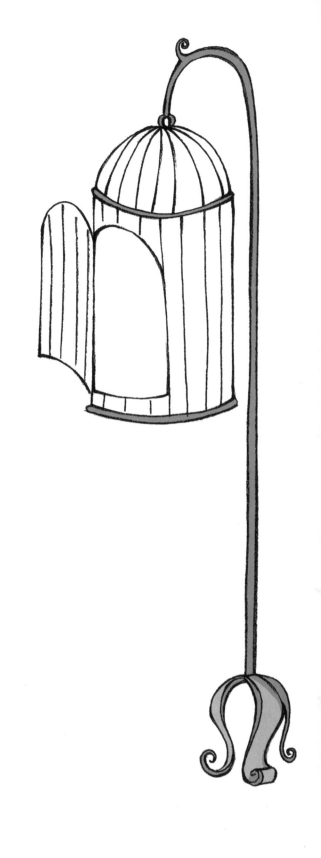

Oh, no—the birds have escaped!

What can you see through the telescope?

Noodles—yum!

Where has the magic carpet taken you?

Mix up a love potion.

Give us glamorous hairstyles.

Paint a masterpiece.

Snowflakes are falling!

What is on these badges?

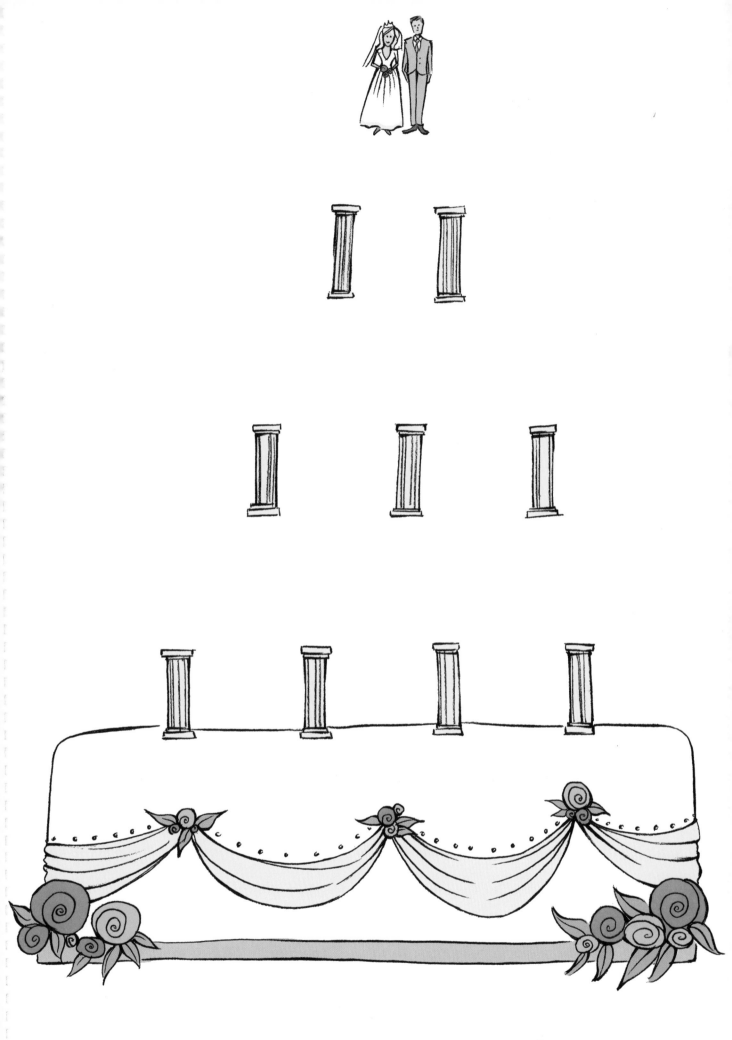

Finish the wedding cake.

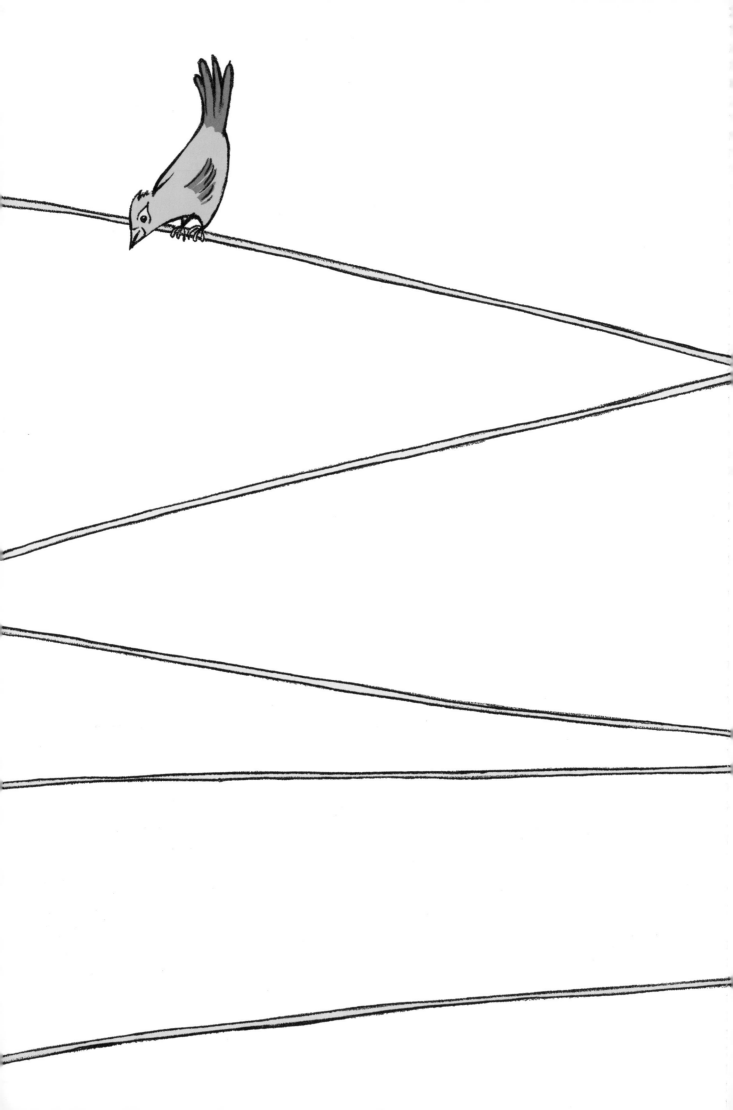

Put some birds on the lines.

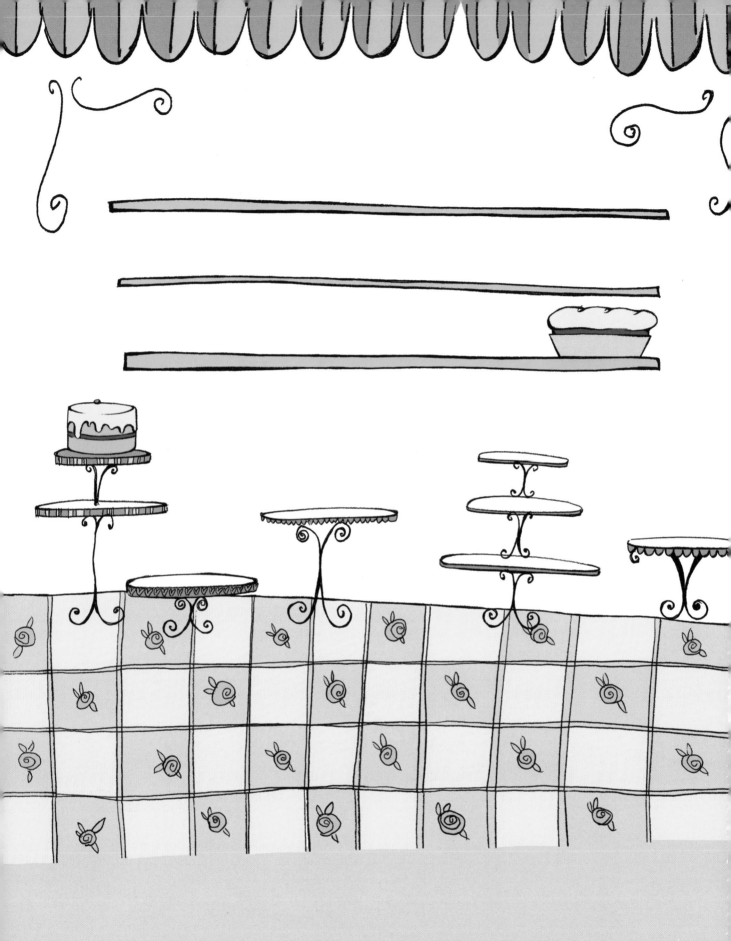

So many delicious cakes!

Make a strawberry sundae.

Fill the shelves and your cart.

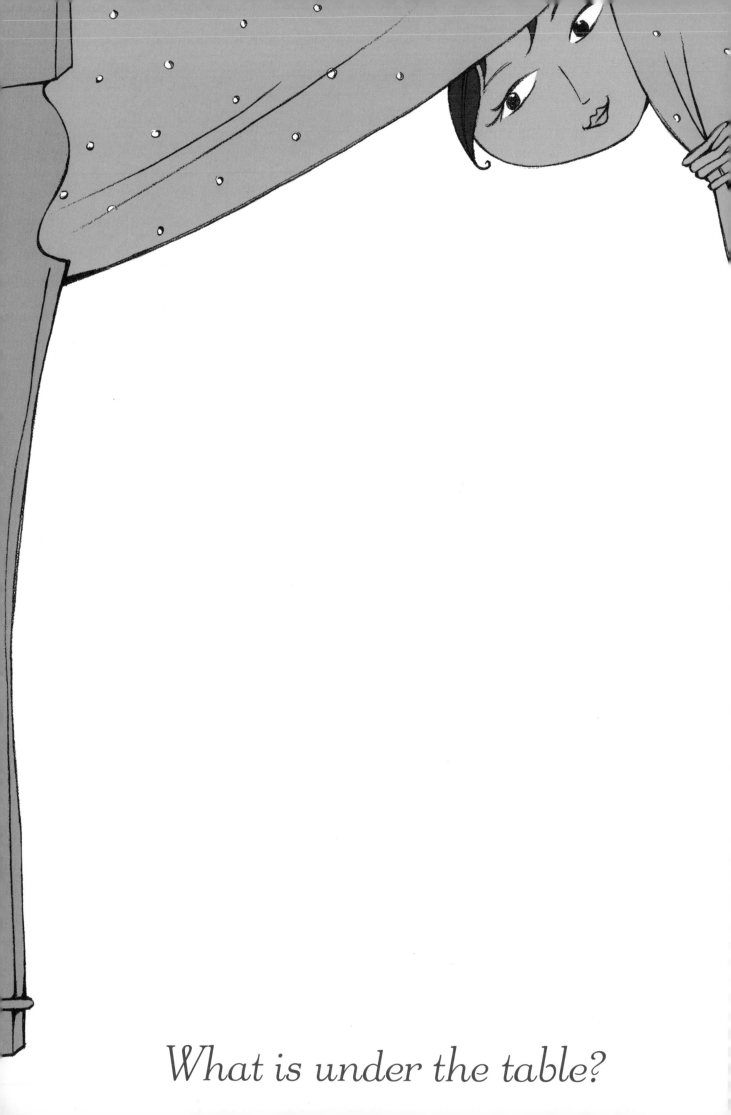

What is under the table?

Decorate the roller skates.

What can you see through
the magic keyhole?

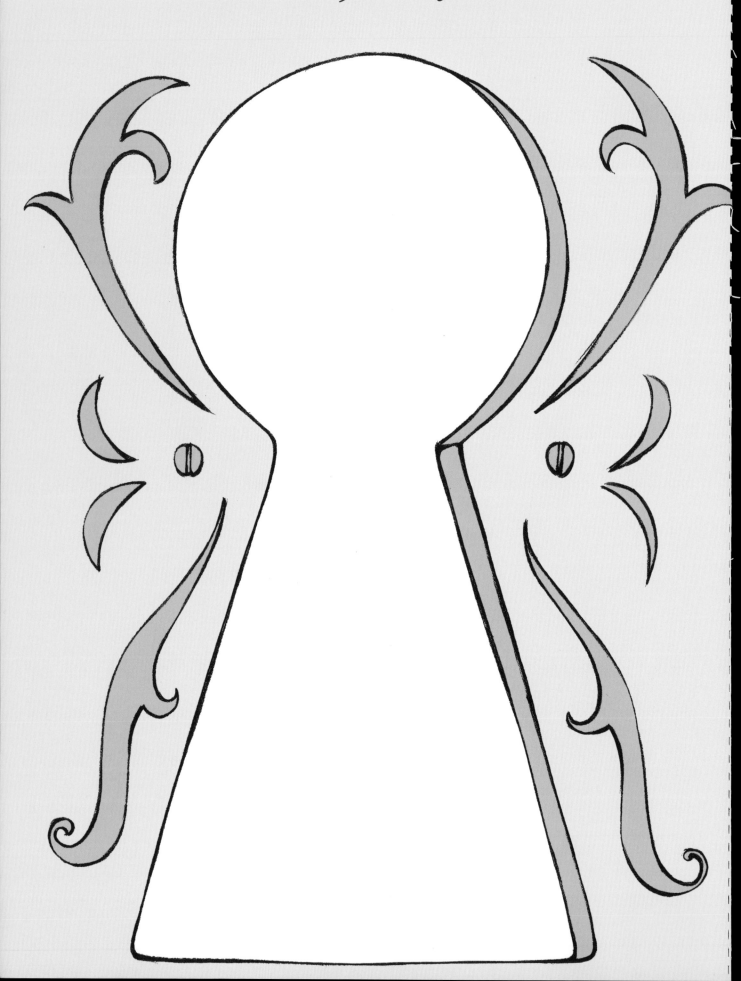

Design some magic keys.

Catch it!

Make an exotic drink.

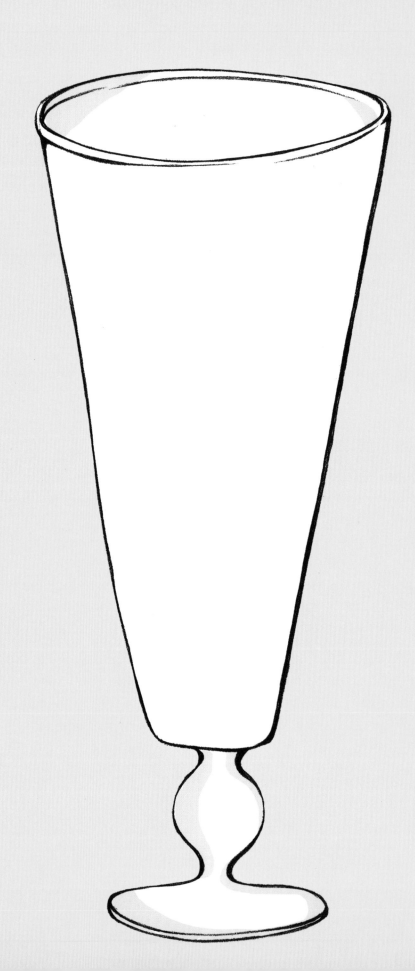

What is on the dressing table?

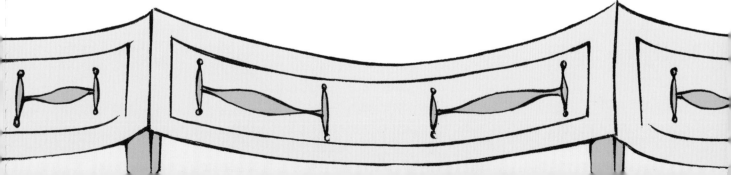

Paint patterns on the plates.

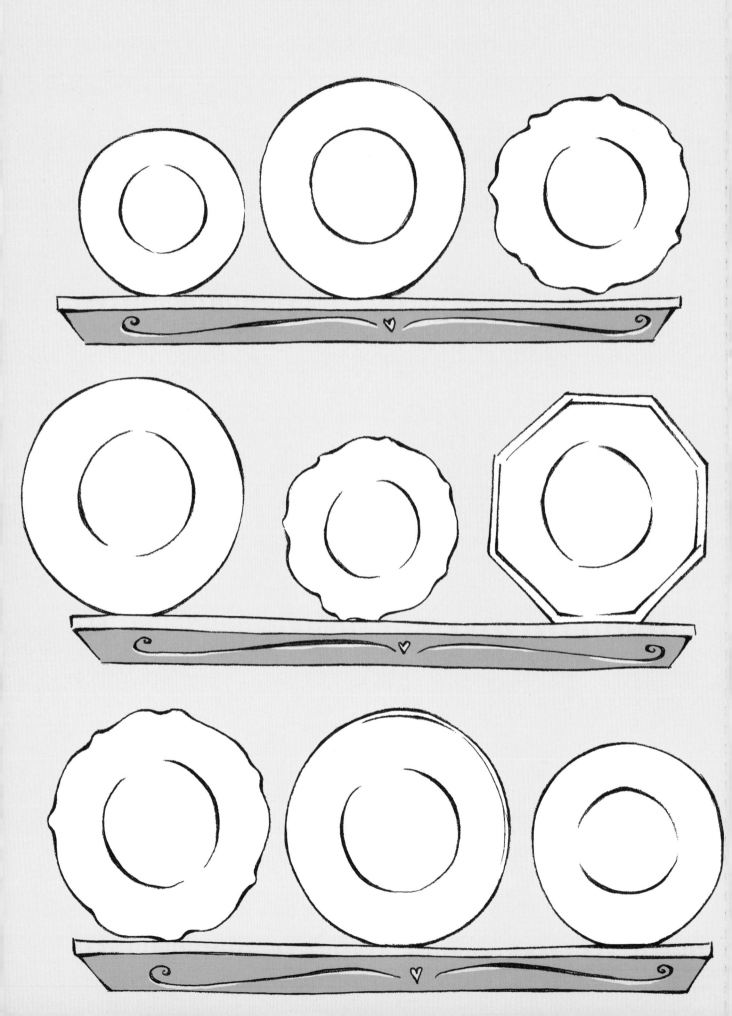

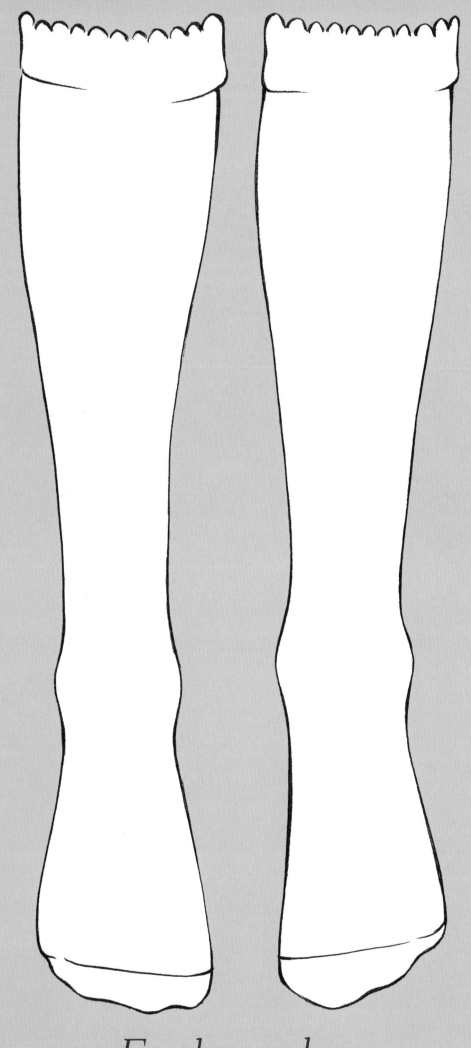

Funky socks.

What is in the rock pools?

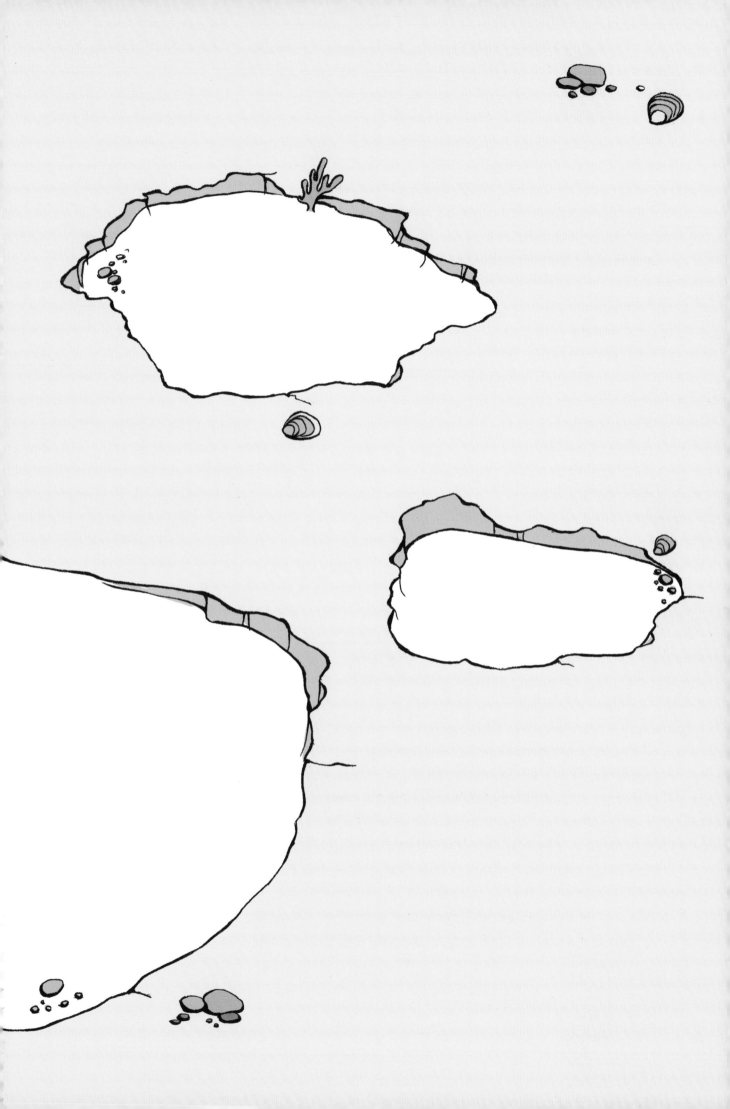

Design a necklace for each of your friends.

Finish the fairies and give them wings.

The latest catwalk fashion.

What is at the end of
the rainbow?

Decorate the tea set.

A beautiful mermaid.

What does the baby need?

Design a card.

What can you see from the plane?

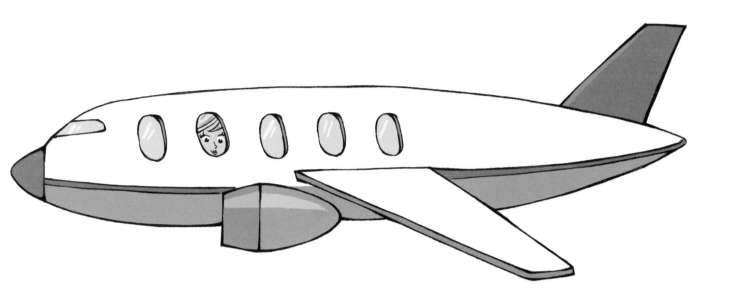

What a beautiful ball gown!

What kind of statue is on the stone?

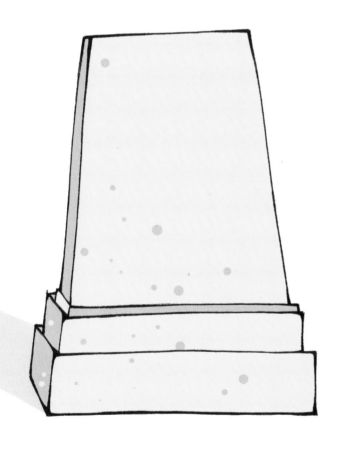

Pillow fight!

What are you knitting?

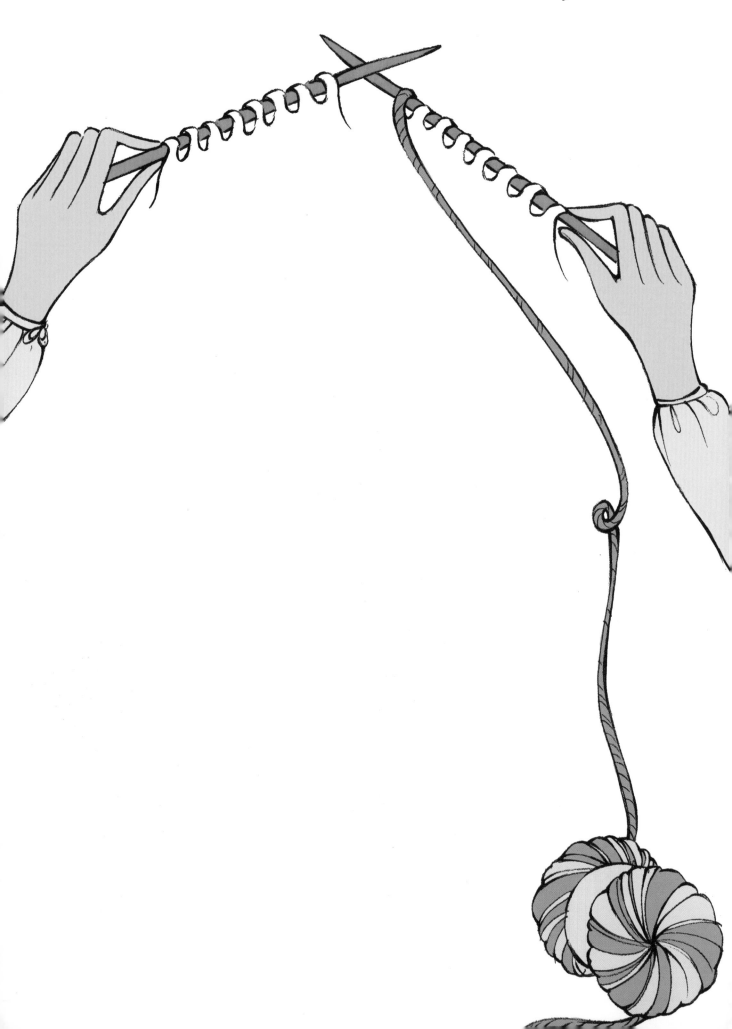

Design some fabulous earrings.

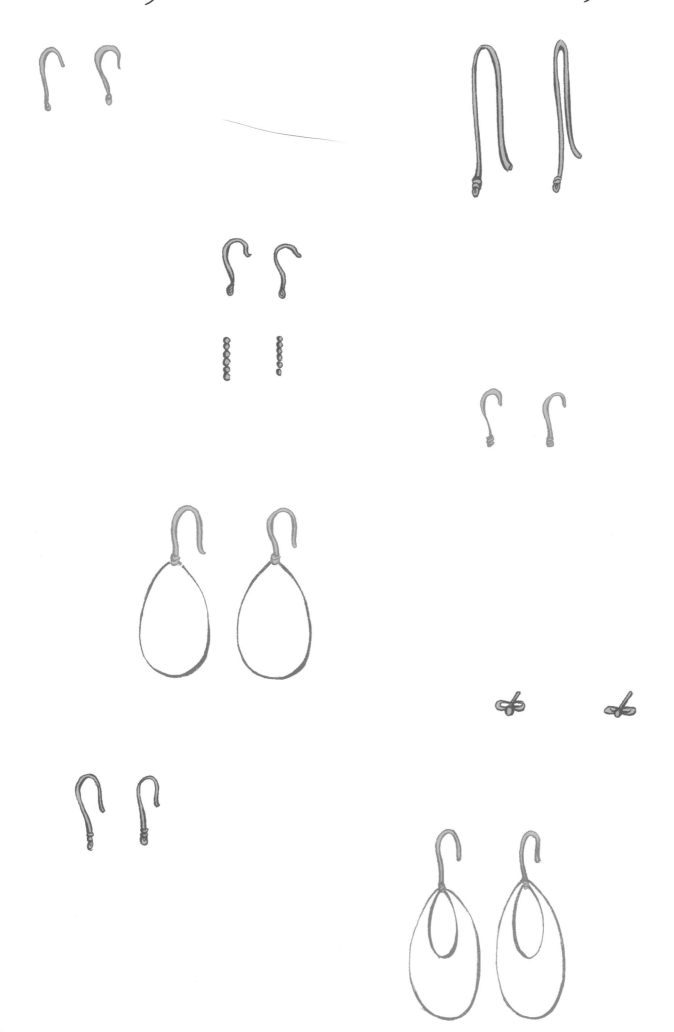

Design the book covers and fill the shelves.

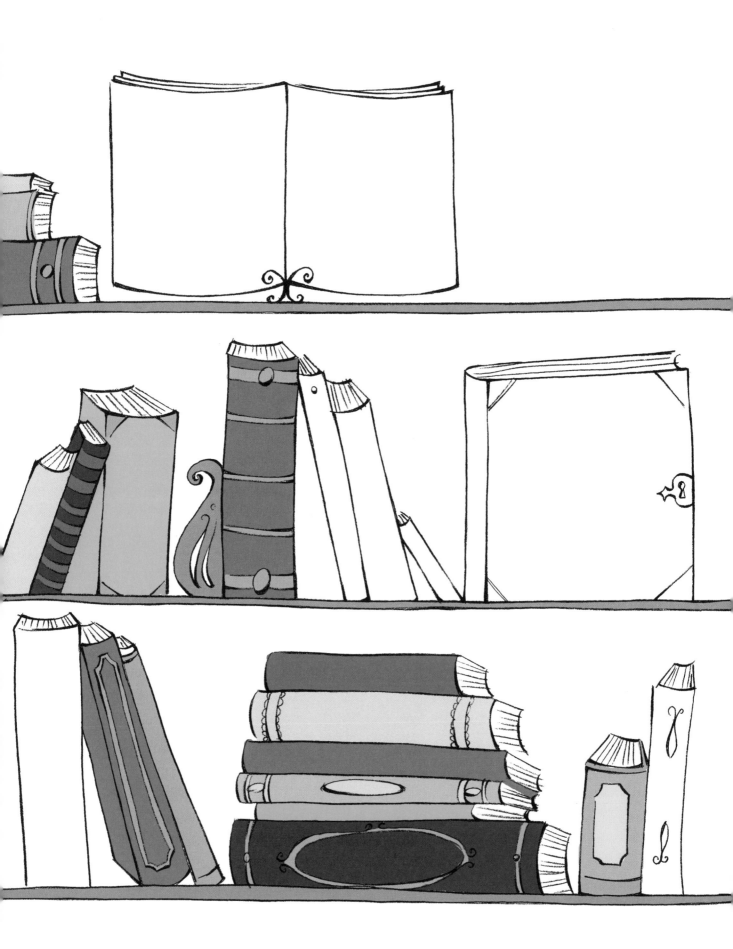

Fill the bagel

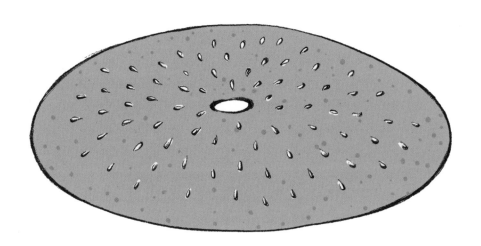

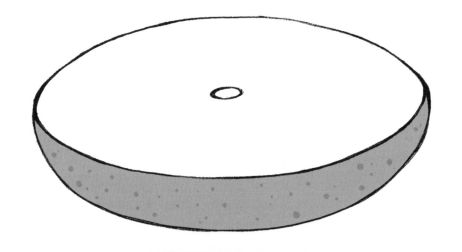

Design some cool album covers.

Mirror, mirror, on the wall . . .

What shapes are the balloons?

Let's go and fly a kite!

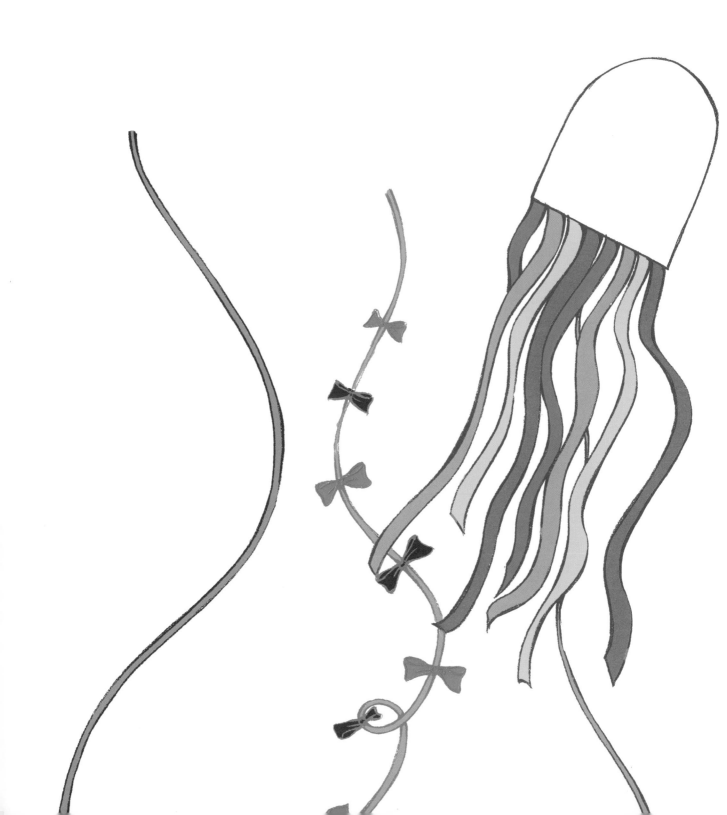

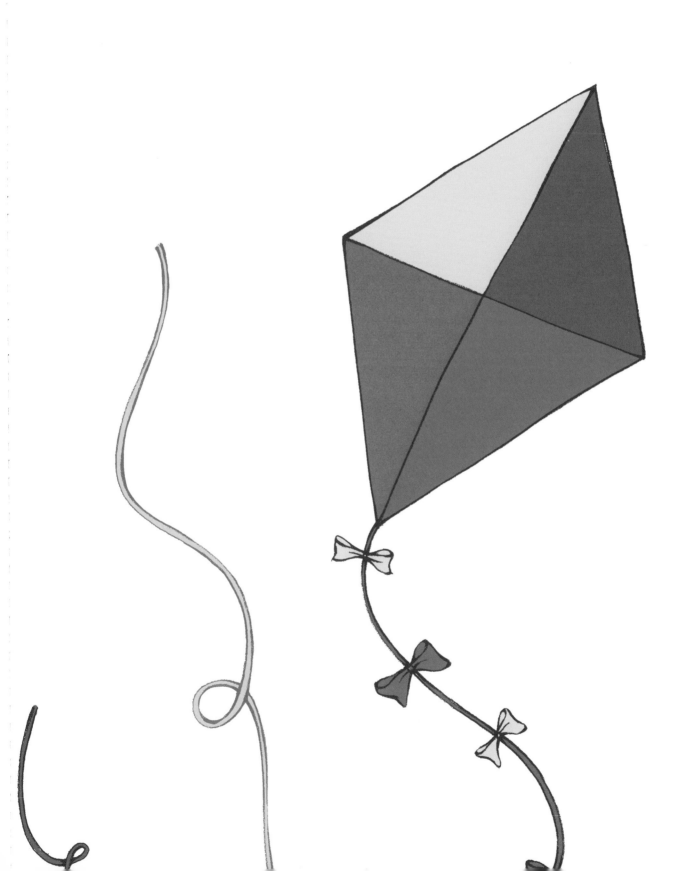

Finish the ballerina.

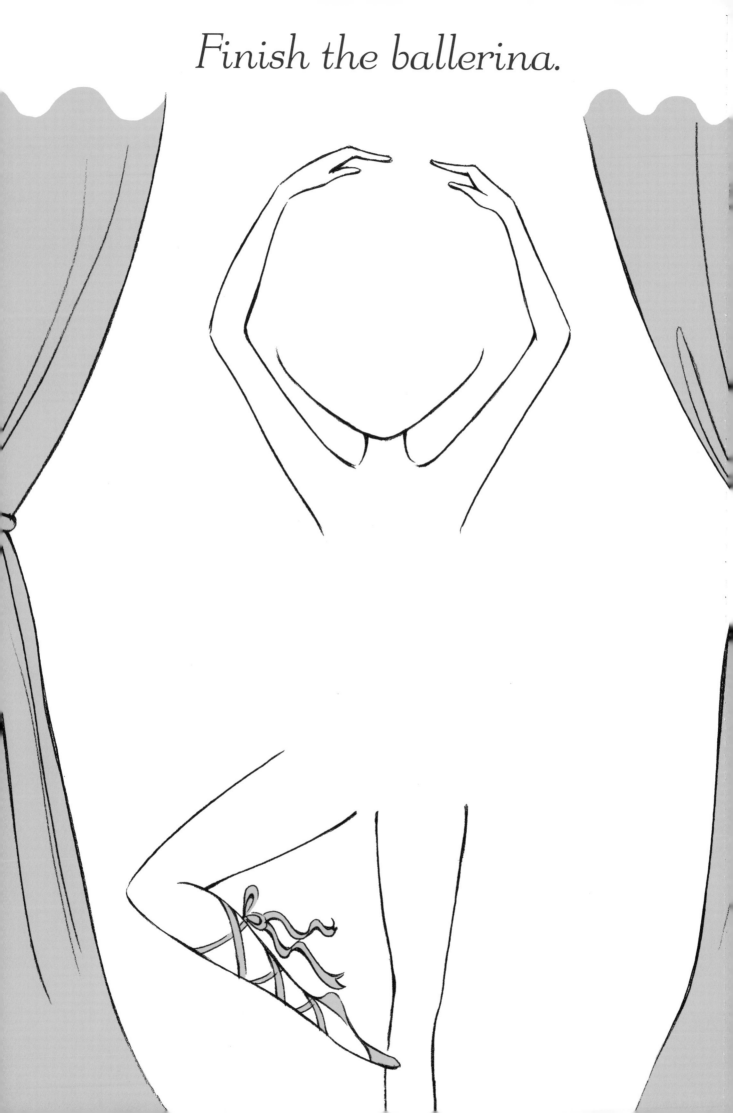

Decorate the wallpaper.

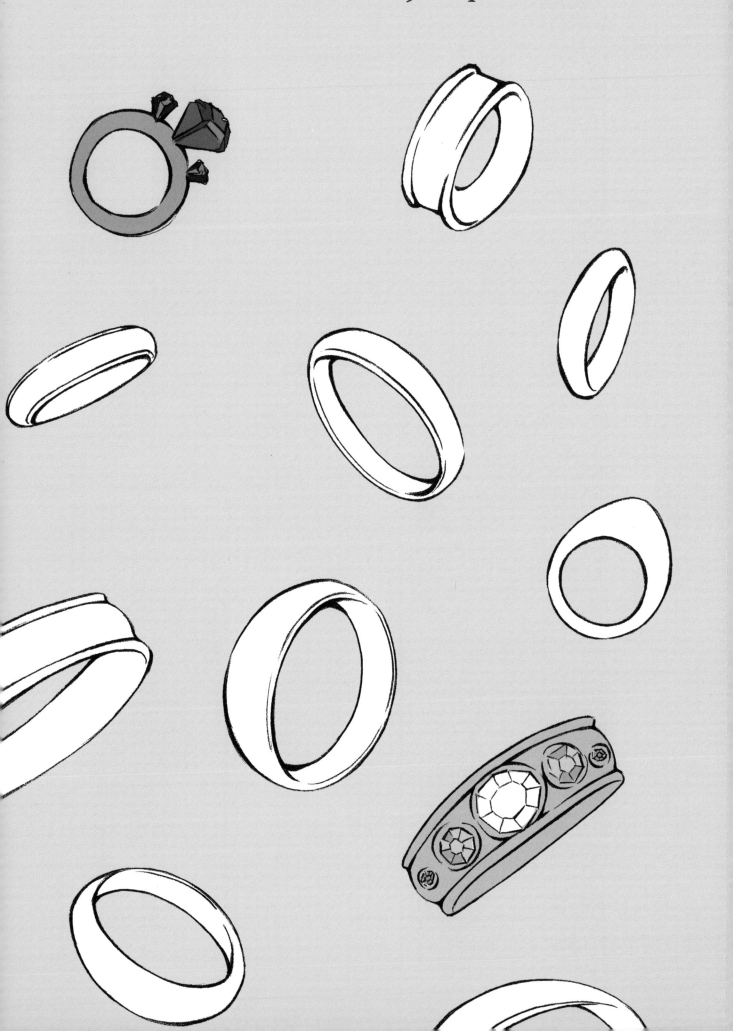

Walk your dogs.

Add lucky charms to the bracelet.

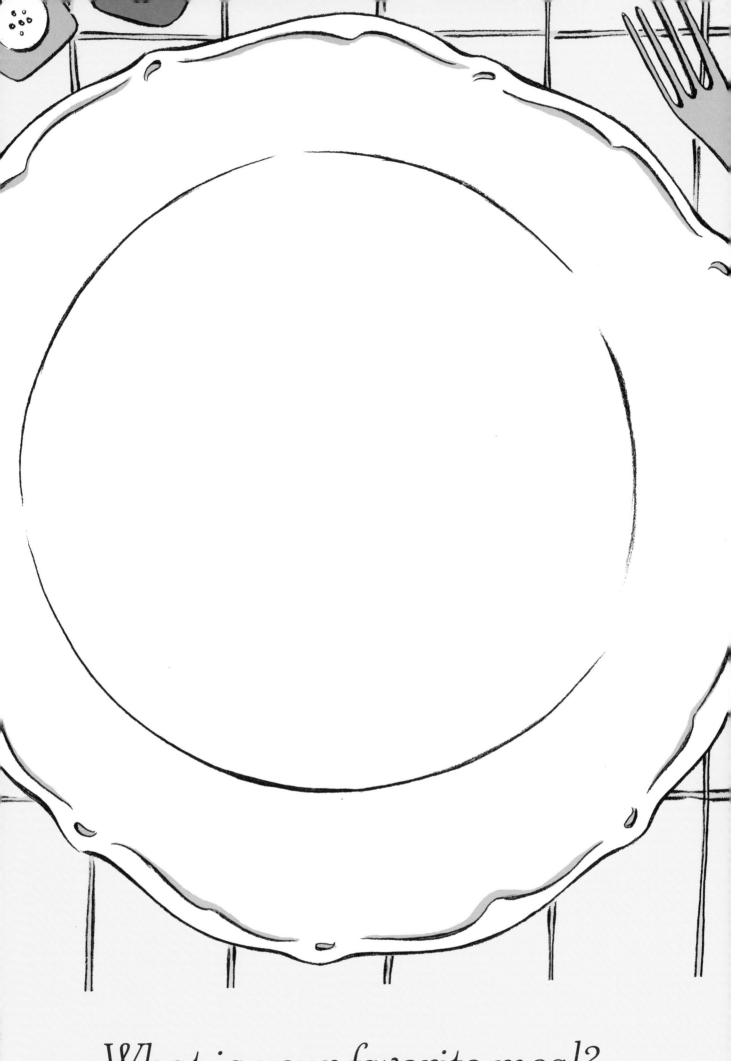

What is your favorite meal?

Design some handbags.

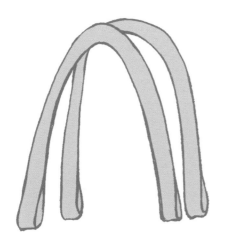

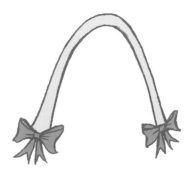

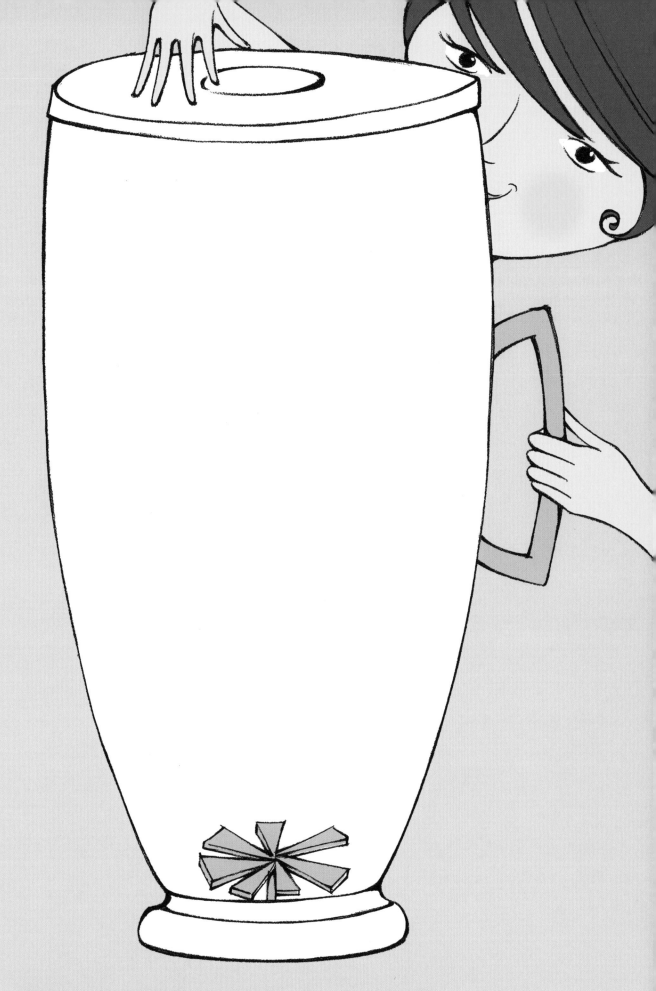

What ingredients are in your favorite smoothie?

What are the teddy bears having
for their picnic?

The perfect ice cream.

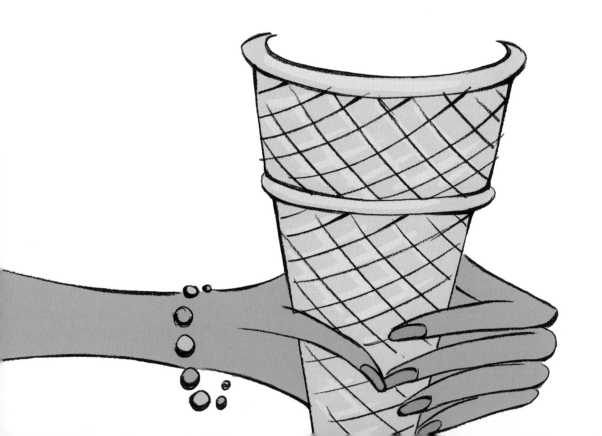

*What can you see from
your hiding place?*

What is in the fridge?

What do you need at the beach?

Where have you landed?

What is for afternoon tea?

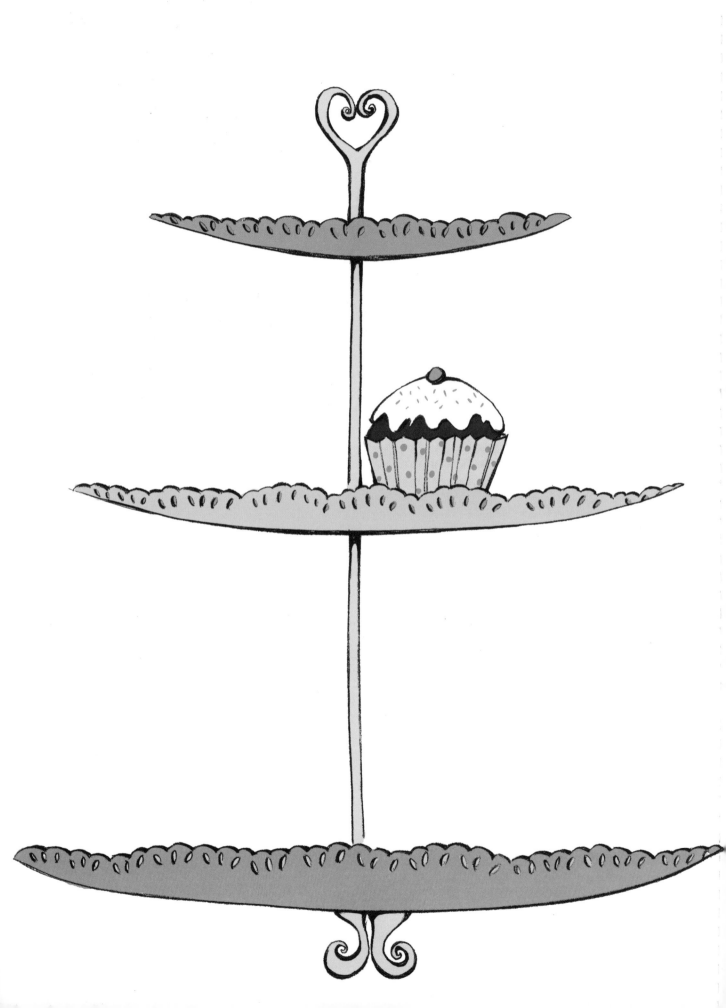

Decorate the umbrellas.

What can you see at
the aquarium?

Who are you talking to?

So many sweets!

What can you pick from the tree?

Design a T-shirt.

Twinkle, twinkle little stars!

What is being performed?

Where are these postcards from?

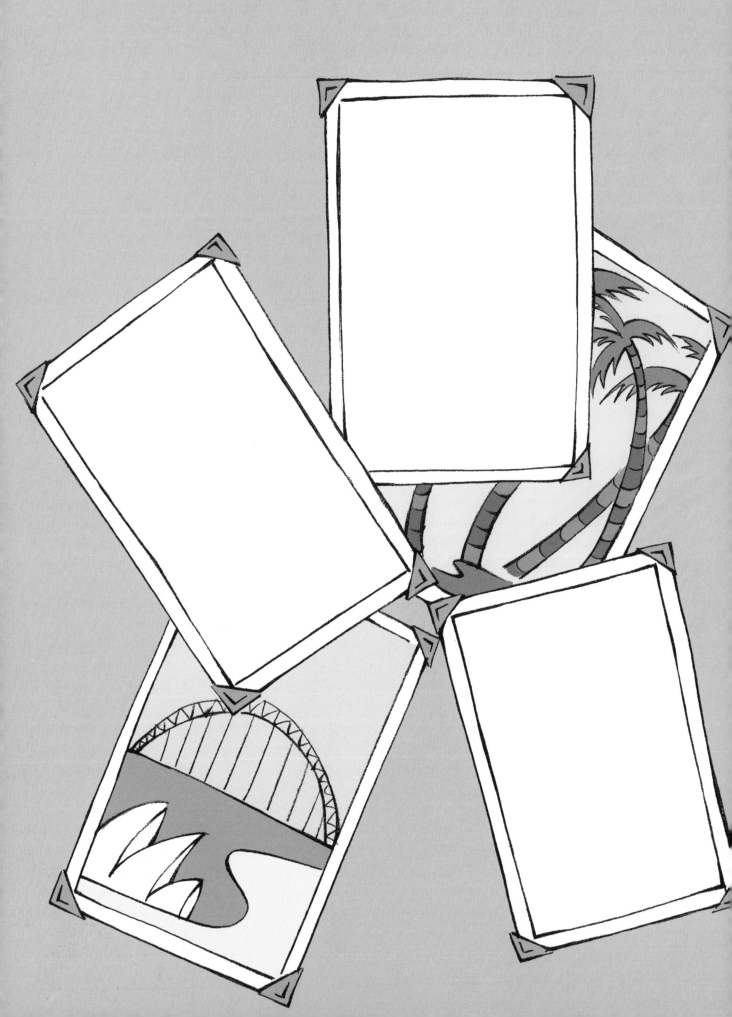

The best snowman ever.

Decorate the shop windows.

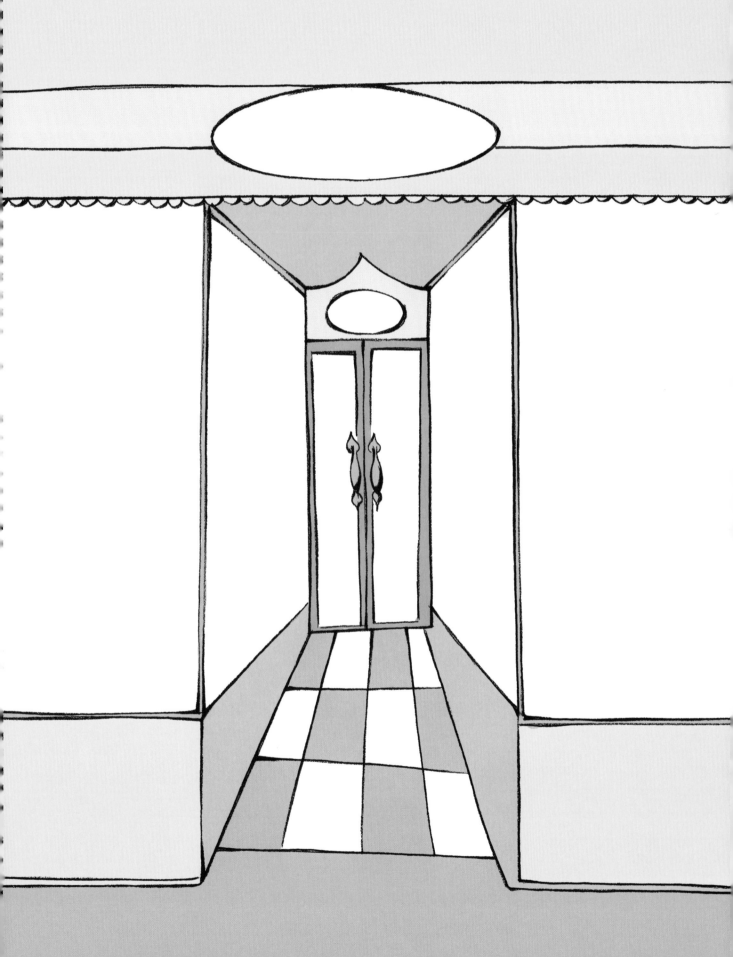

Lots of love.

Finish the Hawaiian necklace.

Design some flip-flops.

What is under the sea?

The secret garden.

Decorate the eggs.

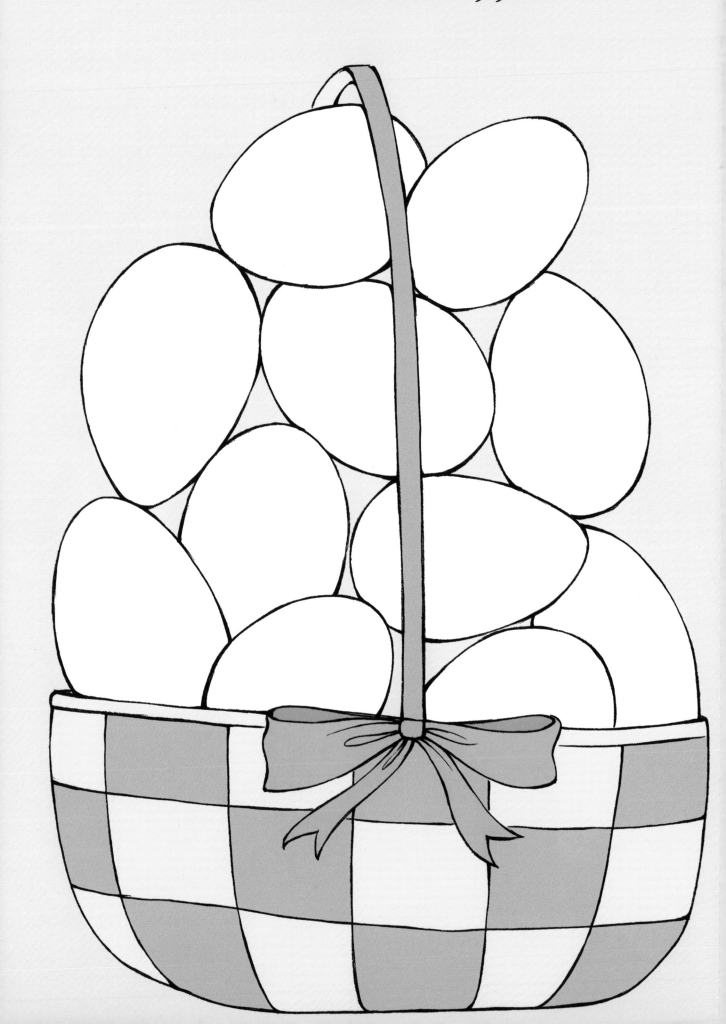

What have you unwrapped?

Ta-da!

Cover the fridge in cool magnets.

Make a wish . . .

and draw it here.

Fill the page with
flowers and hummingbirds.

What treasures can you find
at the garage sale?

Finish the precious tiaras.

Paint the horses in pretty colors.

"I'm forever blowing bubbles . . ."

Build a beautiful sand castle.

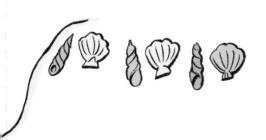

Give the unicorns horns . . .

and fill the meadow with flowers.

What can you see in the clouds?

Finish these wibbly-wobbly jelly creations.

Cover the page in bright,
beautiful buttons and beads.

Fill the night sky with shooting stars . . .

and a big, beautiful moon.

Grow more sunflowers.

Write a message in the sand.
Quick! Before the tide comes in!

What kind of pot has she made?

Fill the pond with pretty fish.

Hang more beautiful bunting
and decorate each triangle.

Fill the cabinet with pretty vases.

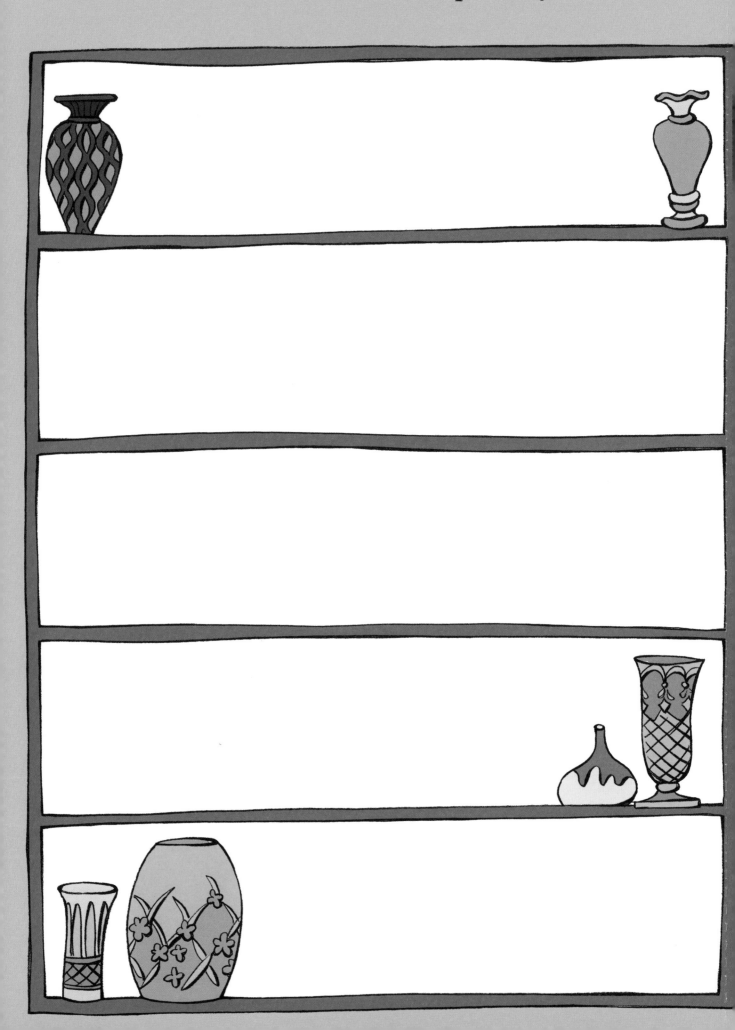

Add more chicks hatching from their shells.

Cover the lake
in lily pads . . .

and add more frogs.

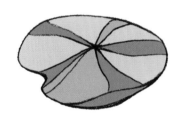

I see seashells on the seashore!

*Sensational
scatter pillows.*

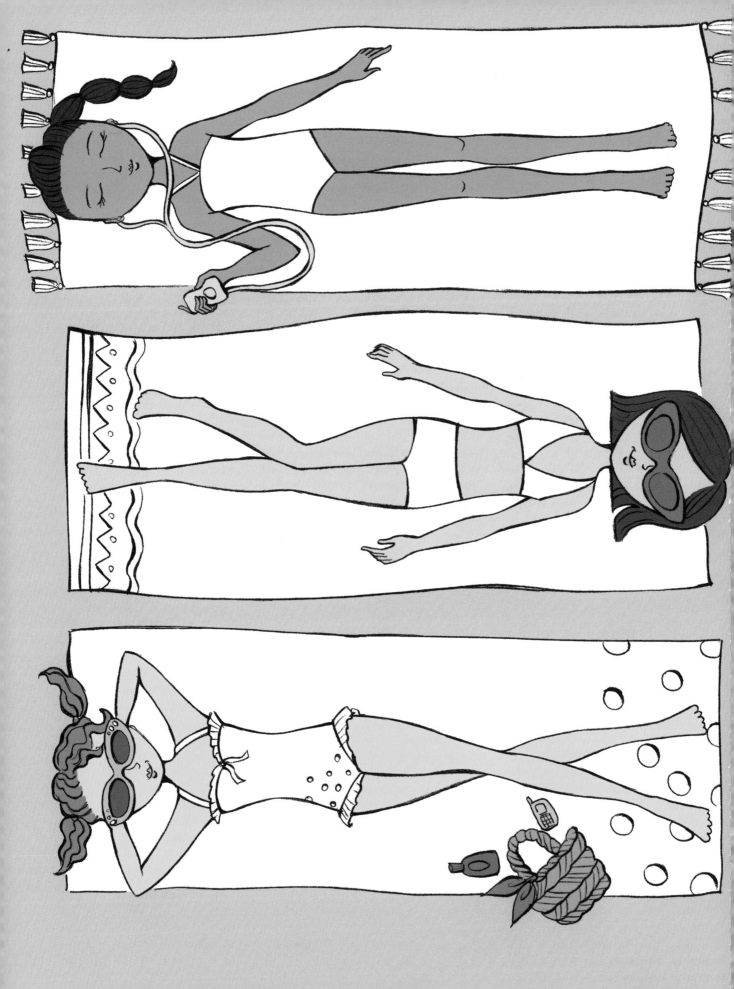

Cover their bathing suits and towels in polka dots.